Put Beginning Readers on the Right Track with
ALL ABOARD READING™

The All Aboard Reading series is especially designed for beginning readers. Written by noted authors and illustrated in full color, these are books that children really *want* to read—books to excite their imagination, expand their interests, make them laugh, and support their feelings. With fiction and nonfiction stories that are high interest and curriculum-related, All Aboard Reading books offer something for every young reader. And with four different reading levels, the All Aboard Reading series lets you choose which books are most appropriate for your children and their growing abilities.

Picture Readers

Picture Readers have super-simple texts, with many nouns appearing as rebus pictures. At the end of each book are 24 flash cards—on one side is a rebus picture; on the other side is the written-out word.

Station Stop 1

Station Stop 1 books are best for children who have just begun to read. Simple words and big type make these early reading experiences more comfortable. Picture clues help children to figure out the words on the page. Lots of repetition throughout the text helps children to predict the next word or phrase—an essential step in developing word recognition.

Station Stop 2

Station Stop 2 books are written specifically for children who are reading with help. Short sentences make it easier for early readers to understand what they are reading. Simple plots and simple dialogue help children with reading comprehension.

Station Stop 3

Station Stop 3 books are perfect for children who are reading alone. With longer text and harder words, these books appeal to children who have mastered basic reading skills. More complex stories captivate children who are ready for more challenging books.

In addition to All Aboard Reading books, look for All Aboard Math Readers™ (fiction stories that teach math concepts children are learning in school); All Aboard Science Readers™ (nonfiction books that explore the most fascinating science topics in age-appropriate language); All Aboard Poetry Readers™ (funny, rhyming poems for readers of all levels); and All Aboard Mystery Readers™ (puzzling tales where children piece together evidence with the characters).

All Aboard for happy reading!

GROSSET & DUNLAP
Published by the Penguin Group
Penguin Group (USA) Inc., 375 Hudson Street, New York, New York 10014, USA
Penguin Group (Canada), 90 Eglinton Avenue East, Suite 700,
Toronto, Ontario M4P 2Y3, Canada
(a division of Pearson Penguin Canada Inc.)
Penguin Books Ltd., 80 Strand, London WC2R 0RL, England
Penguin Group Ireland, 25 St. Stephen's Green, Dublin 2, Ireland
(a division of Penguin Books Ltd.)
Penguin Group (Australia), 250 Camberwell Road, Camberwell, Victoria 3124, Australia
(a division of Pearson Australia Group Pty. Ltd.)
Penguin Books India Pvt. Ltd., 11 Community Centre, Panchsheel Park,
New Delhi—110 017, India
Penguin Group (NZ), 67 Apollo Drive, Rosedale, North Shore 0632, New Zealand
(a division of Pearson New Zealand Ltd.)
Penguin Books (South Africa) (Pty.) Ltd., 24 Sturdee Avenue,
Rosebank, Johannesburg 2196, South Africa

Penguin Books Ltd., Registered Offices:
80 Strand, London WC2R 0RL, England

Library of Congress Cataloging-in-Publication Data

Sloate, Susan.
Pardon that turkey : how thanksgiving became a holiday / by Susan Sloate ;
illustrated by Christian Slade.   p. cm.
ISBN 978-0-448-45347-7 (pbk.)
1. Thanksgiving Day--Juvenile literature. 2. Thanksgiving Day. 3. Holidays.
I. Slade, Christian. II. Title.
GT4975.S59 2010
394.2649--dc22
                                    2009045219

ISBN 978-0-448-45347-7   10 9 8 7 6 5 4 3 2 1

Pardon That Turkey

How Thanksgiving Became a Holiday

by Susan Sloate
illustrated by Christian Slade

Grosset & Dunlap
An Imprint of Penguin Group (USA) Inc.

Chapter One

A National Thanksgiving

Think about the first Thanksgiving. We all know the story.

In the fall of 1620, the Pilgrims came to America from England. Their ship, the *Mayflower*, landed in Cape Cod Bay in Massachusetts. It seemed like a good place to live, and the Pilgrims decided to name their new home Plymouth. But starting a new life was hard work, and the winter was cold and terrible. Many of the Pilgrims didn't live through it. The following autumn, the settlers who had survived that first year in Plymouth gathered together to feast and give thanks.

Today we give thanks just like the

Pilgrims, with a big, special meal. We eat until we can hardly move, filling up on sweet potatoes, corn, stuffing, cranberry sauce, gravy, biscuits, and rich desserts. And, of course, we have a big Thanksgiving turkey.

While we eat, we think about the Pilgrims. After all, they *are* the reason we have a holiday to celebrate, right?

As it turns out, that's not entirely true. Our holiday does honor that first feast, but

the fact that we *have* a national holiday at all
is the work of one special woman. Her name
was Sarah Josepha Hale.

Back in Sarah's time, there was no
national Thanksgiving. Many towns did
celebrate a day of thanks, but in different
ways and on different days. President George
Washington had tried to create a national
Thanksgiving in 1789, but it hadn't lasted.

Sarah thought all Americans should celebrate together. And she was just the person to make it happen! But it wouldn't be easy. For seventeen years, she wrote letters and magazine articles about Thanksgiving. Finally someone agreed with her, and Thanksgiving as we know it came to be.

Today Thanksgiving is celebrated on the same day by the whole country. There is even a national turkey—who gets a pardon from the president! And it's all thanks to the woman who spent her life fighting so that we could give thanks.

• Chapter Two •

A Late Bloomer

Sarah was born on a farm in Newport,
New Hampshire, on October 24, 1788.
She was the third of four children born to
Captain Gordon Buell and his wife, Martha.
Newport was a very small settlement, and the
school was not very good, so Sarah's mother
taught her children at home. Sarah learned a
great deal from her that girls were not usually
taught in those days. Most girls learned only
sewing, cooking, and housekeeping. But
Sarah's mother taught her to read and write
well, and gave her a lifelong love of books,
songs, and poetry.

Although Sarah loved all of her siblings, she was closest to her second brother, Horatio. When Horatio was old enough, he went to study at Dartmouth College. Sarah stayed home with her mother. Being a girl, no one thought she needed a college education. But Horatio knew that Sarah was smart. When he came home from college, he taught her Latin, math, and the other subjects he had learned. And so Sarah got a college education without ever setting foot in a classroom.

When Sarah turned eighteen, she began teaching at the village school in Newport. This was a big change for the town. Back then, only men taught school! But Sarah was determined. She proved to the school board how much she knew and asked them to let her try. She did so well that she worked as a teacher for seven years!

During this time, Sarah's father opened the Rising Sun Tavern on Main Street in Newport. It was there in 1811 that Sarah met David Hale, a young lawyer from a nearby village. David had come to Newport to open a law office, and he and Sarah became friends at once. Two years later, they were married.

Like her brother, David knew how smart Sarah was. After their wedding, they began to study together for two hours every night. They learned French, geology, and botany– the science of plants and flowers. And they read all kinds of books together. When Sarah began to write poetry and short stories, David offered to help her. Instead of the fancy style and big words she had always used, he showed

her how to write simply and directly. Easier words and a simpler style meant that more readers could understand what she had to say.

Sarah and David had a very happy life together. But in September of 1822, after nine years of marriage, David fell ill and died. Two weeks later, his last child was born.

Sarah never got over her grief. In fact, she wore black mourning dresses for the rest of her life. But she knew she had to be strong and figure out how to make a living. After all, she now had five children and very little money. She had to find a way to support her family.

Sarah tried sewing hats at home, but
she wasn't very good and hated it. Working
day after day with her hands wasn't for her.
At night, she kept busy by writing poetry, and
even began a novel. Sarah published her first
book of poetry in 1823. She was proud of
her work, but most readers did not like
it. Then, five years after David's death, she
published her first novel, *Northwood*. It was
a huge success!

Sarah received many letters about her novel. She even got an offer to become the editor of *Ladies' Magazine,* a new magazine for women. Sarah accepted, and she and her children moved to Boston.

Sarah Hale was forty years old, and her real career was just beginning.

• Chapter Three •

Sarah Picks Up Her Pen

For the next nine years, Sarah worked
as the editor of *Ladies' Magazine*. She was the
first woman in the country to be editor of a
magazine. *Ladies' Magazine* had something to
interest every kind of woman. It had pictures
of beautiful clothes, recipes, and ideas on
how to improve the home. As the editor, it
was Sarah's job to decide what to include
in each issue.

But Sarah had something to say, too. And
the magazine was the perfect way to be heard.
As the editor, she could write about the things
that were important to her. Sometimes she
wrote about women's education. Other times

she wrote about the need for more female doctors or more space for children to play.

Sarah became well-known and respected. Her readers listened to her and began to fight for her causes, too. Instead of believing that their only job was to stay at home and care for their children, women began to believe what Sarah told them. They believed that they could make a difference in the world.

In 1837, Sarah left *Ladies' Magazine*
to work as the editor of *Godey's Lady's Book.*
Godey's was the most popular magazine in
the country. Like *Ladies' Magazine*, it had
pictures of clothes, recipes, and home
ideas. It also had short stories by famous
writers of the time, such as Edgar Allan
Poe, Harriet Beecher Stowe, and Nathaniel
Hawthorne. At *Godey's*, Sarah could reach
even more people with her writing.

Sarah didn't just write articles for the magazine, though. She wrote more novels and children's books. She wrote more poetry. She even wrote one of the most famous children's verses in the English language: *Mary Had a Little Lamb*.

But Sarah wanted to do more than just write. She wanted to make a difference. And she knew just how to do it. Sarah had felt for a long time that it was important for America to have a national day for giving thanks. In 1846, she finally decided to fight for the cause.

Sarah knew she might have to wait some time for her dream to come true. But she never dreamed that she would have to wait seventeen years!

Chapter Four

The Thanksgiving Crusade

Sarah began her fight for a national Thanksgiving by writing articles in *Godey's*. She told her readers what a good idea it would be and asked for their support. She even wrote articles describing wonderful dishes and fun family games for such a holiday. But as years passed with no change, she decided to do more.

→ Sarah began to write to politicians around the country, explaining why she thought the holiday was needed. Over the years, she wrote thousands of these letters. And she encouraged *Godey's* readers to write to *their* local politicians, too. Sarah's readers

were very loyal to her. Thousands of them
wrote letters, just as she'd asked. They told
their politicians they wanted to celebrate a
day of giving thanks.

The politicians listened. One by one,
they began to declare a day of celebration
for their states. Not every state recognized the
holiday, of course, but a lot of them agreed
to do it.

But this was still not enough for Sarah. Slavery and other issues were tearing the Northern and Southern states apart. It seemed as though the country would soon split in two. Sarah knew that a national Thanksgiving was now more important than ever. She believed that celebrating a holiday together would be the best way to keep the union whole.

So she picked up her pen again. This time she wrote directly to the president of the United States, Zachary Taylor. She asked him to declare one day each year for the country to give thanks together.

But President Taylor was busy with other matters. The country was facing a crisis, and he did not have time to bother with a holiday. He wrote her back and told her no.

Sarah did not give up. When President Taylor left office, she wrote to the new president, Millard Fillmore. But President Fillmore did not consider a Thanksgiving holiday very important, either.

Sarah was probably upset by his response, but she didn't let it stop her. Deep down, she was sure that the key to a national Thanksgiving was getting the president to agree. When Franklin Pierce was elected president, she wrote another letter.

President Pierce said no to her, too. Sarah waited until he left office and tried again with the next president, James Buchanan.

By now the country was ready to break apart. Southerners felt people in the North did not understand them or their way of life. They thought they would be better off starting their own country. It seemed like the only way to settle the issue would be with a war.

Sarah explained to President Buchanan that a national day of thanks would help bring people together. But he did not agree with her.

Sarah still did not give up.

In 1861, the Union came apart. The Southern states broke away and formed the Confederate States of America. A civil war had begun.

As the years of war rolled by, Sarah wrote a letter to yet another president–the fifth since she had begun fighting for her cause. This time the letter went to Abraham Lincoln. Sarah pointed out that now was the best time to declare a day of thanksgiving. Reminding people of their blessings could help the Union come back together.

President Lincoln saw her point. The country *did* need something to help pull it together. In 1863, he declared Thanksgiving a national holiday. It would be celebrated every year on the last Thursday in November.

After seventeen years and thousands of letters to presidents, congressmen, and local

officials, Sarah's fight had come to an end.
She had begun her cause at the age of fifty-eight
with no more than an idea. By the time it was
over, she was seventy-five.

Few women ever accomplished as much
as Sarah did. She wrote fiction and poetry,

including a verse that is still recited today. She saw opportunities for women increase, in large part because of the articles she had written over the years. She was the driving force behind two great magazines.

But none of her accomplishments took her longer to achieve, or made her prouder, than the creation of a national Thanksgiving holiday.

Of course, Thanksgiving isn't a happy time for *everyone* . . .

Chapter Five

The Start of a Tradition

Although Thanksgiving is only one day long, people celebrate it as part of a four-day holiday. The holiday begins on Thursday and goes through the weekend. It's a time to get together with friends and family, and to give thanks for the year. And, of course, it's the time to enjoy a big Thanksgiving feast. At the center of it all is a giant turkey! But not every turkey raised each year becomes dinner.

Some time after President Lincoln created a national Thanksgiving, a new tradition began. According to the tradition, one turkey out of the millions raised that year will receive a

"pardon" from the president of the United States. That means the turkey's life is saved. Instead of becoming dinner, he gets sent to a nearby petting farm. (The president has the power to pardon people for their crimes, so why not turkeys?)

This tradition started many years ago. There is even a story that President Lincoln himself gave the first pardon to the first turkey. This makes sense since he was the president who declared Thanksgiving a holiday.

The story says that President Lincoln's youngest son, ten-year-old Tad, had a pet turkey named Jack. The turkey had been given to the president, and he had turned it over to his son.

When Thanksgiving became a holiday, Tad realized that his pet turkey might turn out to be his holiday dinner. He didn't like that idea at all!

Tad burst into President Lincoln's office in the middle of an important meeting and asked his father if he would please spare Jack's life. The president enjoyed granting his sons' requests, and he happily agreed.

Months later, during the election of 1864, the president saw Jack strutting around by the voting booths at the White House. President Lincoln asked Tad, "What business has the turkey stalking about the polls in that way? Does he vote?"

"No," Tad is supposed to have said. "He's not of age."

The story of Tad's turkey is fun, but it may not be true. Some versions say that Jack was not a turkey at all, but a toy soldier. The doll was sent as a gift to Tad by the Sanitary Commission in New York.

According to this story, Tad was playing with Jack, his brothers, and some friends. The boys apparently decided that Jack was disobeying military law. Once again, the Lincoln boys asked their father to pardon

Jack. In this version of the story, President Lincoln actually wrote a note that said, "The doll Jack is pardoned by order of the President."

There is no evidence that either story is true, but the tradition of "pardoning" one turkey every Thanksgiving has gone on through the years.

• Chapter Six •

The Truth of the Matter

So, where did the turkey pardoning tradition *really* begin?

Lots of people think it started with Harry Truman, but that isn't exactly true.

The National Turkey Federation (NTF) *did* give President Truman a turkey in 1947. It was the first time the NTF had ever given a bird to any president, and it was the start of a very real tradition. Every year since then, the NTF has given the president and his family a holiday turkey.

But President Truman did not pardon the turkey he was given. In fact, the bird was given to him on December 15 and was meant

for Christmas dinner, not Thanksgiving.
There is no proof that President Truman ever
pardoned a Thanksgiving turkey, or even
thought of pardoning one.

Then in November of 1963, President
John F. Kennedy was presented with his
Thanksgiving turkey in the Rose Garden
of the White House. Although President

Kennedy said that he did not intend to eat
the bird, he never said he was pardoning it.
Even so, the next day, the newspapers said
the turkey had been "pardoned."

In 1987, President Ronald Reagan joked
at a press conference that if his Thanksgiving
turkey were not already intended for a petting
farm, "I would have pardoned him."

But the real beginning of the pardoning
tradition started with President George H.W.
Bush. President Bush was presented with his

first turkey in 1989, during his first year in the White House. The president thanked the NTF and said "Let me assure you–and this fine tom turkey–that he will not end up on anyone's dinner table. Not this guy. He's been granted a presidential pardon as of right now, allowing him to live out his days on a farm not far from here."

It was the first serious mention of a turkey pardon by a president, and is the beginning of the tradition as we know it today. President Bush pardoned a Thanksgiving turkey every year that he was in office. And every president since has continued the custom.

Today, the National Turkey Federation presents four turkeys to the president. Two are ready-to-eat turkeys, which become the president's Thanksgiving dinner. The other two are live birds. The first is the National Turkey, who gets pardoned in a big, public ceremony. The other is the Alternate National Turkey, who steps in if the first bird can't fulfill his duties. Of course, the National Turkey

doesn't *really* have any duties. After the "pardon," both birds are sent to live out their lives in a petting zoo or on a farm. Since 2005, the turkeys have gone somewhere even more special. They have been sent to Disneyland in California to be Grand Marshals of the Disneyland Thanksgiving Day parade!

Not all turkeys get their own parade, though. In 2007, more than 271 million turkeys were raised in the US, and 235 million of them were eaten. About forty-six million of them were eaten at Thanksgiving alone. In fact, nearly 88 percent of Americans report that they eat turkey at Thanksgiving. Another twenty-two million turkeys were eaten at Christmas and nineteen million at Easter.

Sarah Hale probably didn't think much about the turkey when she fought for a national day of thanksgiving. She thought only about the importance of giving thanks for our blessings and how that could bring together a nation that was falling apart.

She worked for seventeen years, wrote thousands of letters herself, got her readers to write thousands more, and personally contacted five different presidents. Today we owe thanks not just for our blessings or to the Pilgrims, but to the remarkable woman who never gave up.

Thank you, Sarah Hale, for using your pen to bring millions of Americans together.